Piece by Piece

Book C

11 LATE ELEMENTARY COLOR PIECES
FOR SOLO PIANO

by Tom Gerou

Foreword

These original piano solos offer students the opportunity to explore a variety of styles, techniques, and moods. Each piece stays within the late elementary level, and the collection explores the various registers of the piano and chromaticism. The pieces require coordination between the hands while avoiding single-hand triads. Challenges include reading in the keys of G major and F major, playing melodic and harmonic intervals up to a 7th, pedaling, and more frequent hand shifts. All of the pieces focus on a melodic or rhythmic idea that enhances a story being told, so lyrics are included to spark imaginative playing. Accompaniments provide rich harmonies and rhythmic motion, although each piece is playable as a solo without the accompaniment.

Alfred Music
P.O. Box 10003
Van Nuys, CA 91410-0003
alfred.com

D1247343

Copyright © 2019 by Alfred Music
All rights reserved. Printed in USA.

No part of this book shall be reproduced, arranged, adapted, recorded, publicly performed, stored in a retrieval system, or transmitted by any means without written permission from the publisher. In order to comply with copyright laws, please apply for such written permission and/or license by contacting the publisher at alfred.com/permissions.

ISBN-10: 1-4706-4135-6
ISBN-13: 978-1-4706-4135-1

Numero Uno

Tom Gerou

Some-times I would like to be the one who's first.

Most times I come in sec-ond, oth-er times in third.

If I try much hard - er, I may just suc - ceed.

No doubt, with per - se - ver - ance, there is not de - feat!

Optional Duet Accompaniment (Student plays one octave higher.)

17 I'm quite good at spell - ing; here I'm at my best.

21 Want to see that grand prize plopped up - on my desk!

25 If I want some rib - bons plas - tered on my wall,

Both hands 8va - - - - - - - - - **D.C. al Fine**

29 I would need to win win - ter, spring, and fall!

D.C. al Fine

Lure of the Mermaids

Tom Gerou

Optional Duet Accompaniment (Student plays one octave higher.)

*Student does not use pedal with duet.

The Brand-New You

Tom Gerou

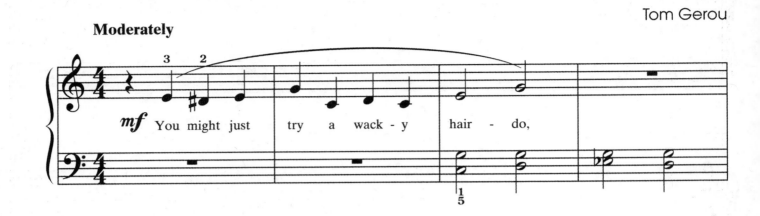

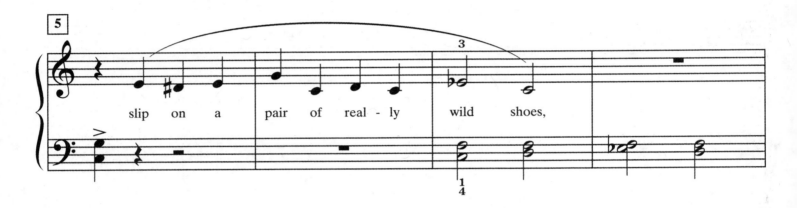

Optional Duet Accompaniment (Student plays one octave higher.)

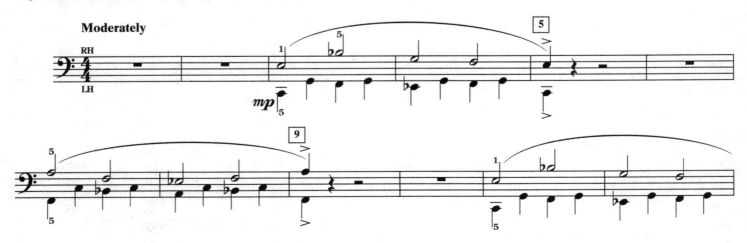

Black Widow's Wedding

Tom Gerou

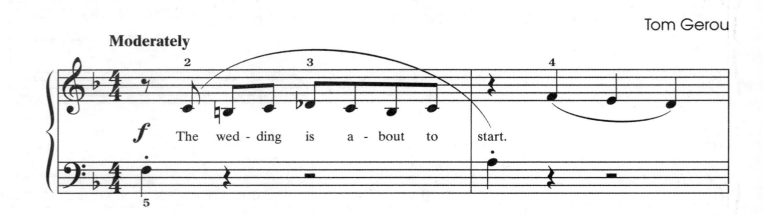

The wed - ding is a - bout to start.

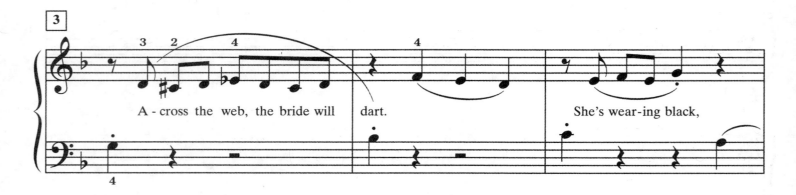

A - cross the web, the bride will dart. She's wear-ing black,

with silk - en hat. She's a stun-ning vi - sion in her gown.

Optional Duet Accompaniment (Student plays one octave higher.)

Rich and Famous

Tom Gerou

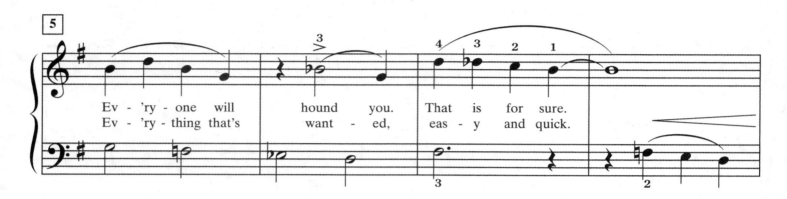

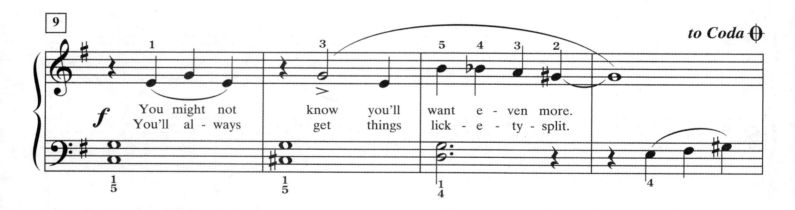

Optional Duet Accompaniment (Student plays one octave higher.)

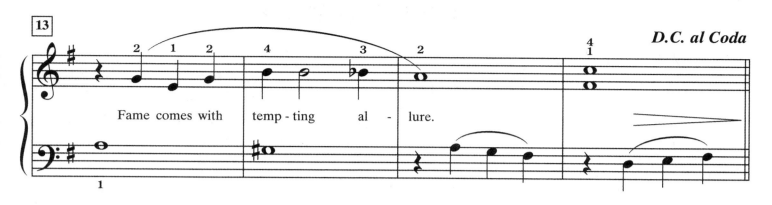

D.C. al Coda

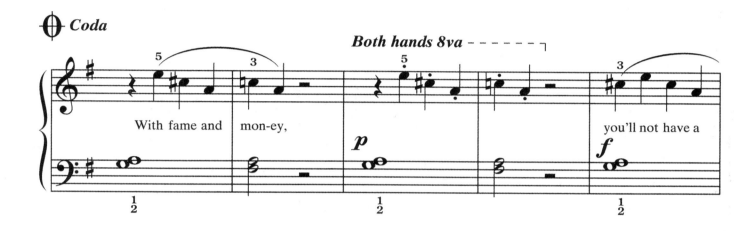

What Is Blue?

Tom Gerou

Optional Duet Accompaniment (Student plays one octave higher.)

Seaside Scavenger

Tom Gerou

Optional Duet Accompaniment (Student plays one octave higher.)

The Gentle Giant

Tom Gerou

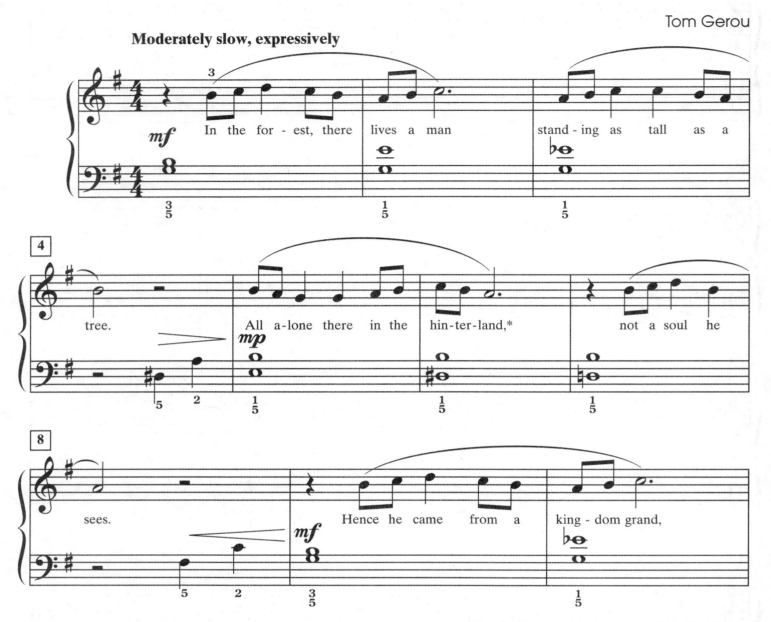

Hinterland is an area lying beyond what is visable or known.

Optional Duet Accompaniment (Student plays one octave higher.)

The Leprechaun

Tom Gerou

Optional Duet Accompaniment (Teacher plays one octave higher.)

Feelin' Terrific

Tom Gerou

Optional Duet Accompaniment (Student plays one octave higher.)

Of Pirates and Gold

Tom Gerou

Optional Duet Accompaniment (Student plays one octave higher.)

Duet Continued

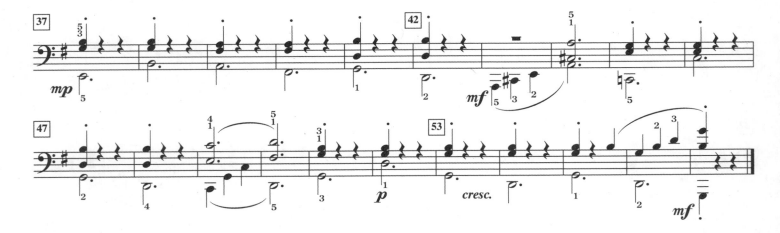